MW01145441

Imagine being a young man grappling with the possibility of the Lord calling you into pastoral ministry. How do you get from where you are today to serving as a pastor someday? *Pathway to Pastoral Ministry* is an indispensable guide for such a person. This treasure trove of wisdom for aspiring pastors provides vital insights and practical advice to help a young man discern God's call in his life. I look forward to giving copies of this book to future pastors for years to come!

—Patrick Odle
President, Baptist Mid-Missions

God loves His church, giving to His church the gifts of Christ— pastors! Dean capably and expertly provides a pathway for those men aspiring to pastoral ministry. This book also is helpful to churches and pastors looking to identify the next generation of shepherds. In *Pathway to Pastoral Ministry*, you will find good theology and practical steps for men sensing the call of God to pastoral ministry. I highly recommend this book. It is a valuable, practical resource for any local church seeking to train the next generation of vocational servants.

—David E. Strope
GARBC Interim National Representative

Pathway to Pastoral Ministry is a must-read for any person with the desire for pastoral ministry. Dean lays out a much-needed biblical and practical approach that brings clarity and direction to the reader. In a world where so many churches are without pastors, this book helps meet the need of the hour. I believe every pastor should read this book and have copies on hand to encourage the next generation for pastoral ministry.

—Jeremy Frazor
President and CEO, Frazor Evangelistic Association

Pathway to Pastoral Ministry is a valuable resource for young men considering pastoral ministry and for pastors training young men pursuing pastoral ministry. Dean shares insights from his own journey into pastoral ministry, offers counsel based on his years of experience as a pastor who equipped young men for ministry, and, most importantly, instructs from Scripture about the call to vocational ministry. One of the key strengths of *Pathway to Pastoral Ministry* is its usefulness as a tool for pastors involved in ministerial training. Pastors can simply assign a few chapters for a young man to read, schedule a meeting to discuss the material, use the questions at the end of each chapter to prompt dialogue, and help the young man evaluate his understanding of ministry, his spiritual maturity, his ministry skills, and his potential next steps.

—Ben Ice
Lead Pastor, Lighthouse Bible Church, Simi Valley, California

Many have noted the dearth of qualified pastors to fill the pulpits of pastorless churches. Where will those men come from, and how will they go from where they are to the pulpit of the church God is preparing for them? While God calls pastors and appoints them to His church, He also uses qualified spiritual mentors to help them recognize His call and prepare them for His service. Dean Taylor is one of those mentors. He has thought deeply and biblically about what it means to be a pastor, and he has exemplified it over many years of faithful pastoral ministry. God has used him to shepherd His church and is now using him to prepare future shepherds for the church. *Pathway to Pastoral Ministry* is an important contribution to that call. It is written to young men who are sensing the possibility that God is setting them apart for pastoral ministry. Instead of slapping them on the back and pushing them blindly down the path, Dean walks beside these young men and helps them recognize important markers on the path that will help confirm God's working in their lives. While they walk together, Dean points out simple but significant ways a young man can prepare his life for pastoral ministry—should God so will. *Pathway to Pastoral Ministry* is a short, practical, and extremely helpful resource for young men, parents, youth pastors, pastors, Christian educators, and ministry mentors who are investing in young men for the sake of the gospel and the good of the Church.

—Sam Horn
Pastor for Preaching and Vision, Palmetto Baptist Church, Piedmont, South Carolina

Pathway to
Pastoral Ministry

FIRST STEPS FOR YOUNG MEN

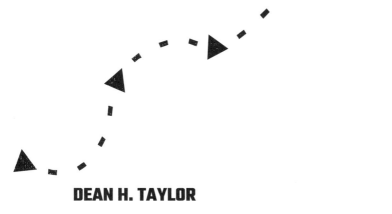

DEAN H. TAYLOR

Unless otherwise indicated Scripture quotations are from The ESV® Bible (The Holy Bible, English Standard Version®), copyright © 2001 by Crossway, a publishing ministry of Good News Publishers. Used by permission. All rights reserved.

Scripture quotations marked NKJV taken from the New King James Version®. Copyright © 1982 by Thomas Nelson. Used by permission. All rights reserved.

ISBN: 978-1-960820-02-0 (hardcover)
ISBN: 978-1-960820-04-4 (paperback)
ISBN: 978-1-960820-03-7 (digital)

Library of Congress Control Number: 2024913791

Front cover image and book design by Lance Young with Higher Rock Creative Studio.

First printing edition 2024.

Faith Publications
1900 NW 4th St.
Ankeny, IA. 50023
faith.edu/publications

Printed in the United States of America

Dedication

With appreciation for my students

and those who will follow in their steps

"That the man of God may be complete,

equipped for every good work."

2 Timothy 3:17

▶ Table of Contents

▶ Introduction

God is calling men to ministry. How do you know if that's you? Maybe you're curious about what it means to be a pastor. What do you do next? You might have a strong desire to pursue ministry. Whom should you talk to?

I've worked through those questions myself, and I've helped numerous young men do the same. I'm glad you are thinking about ministry, and I'd love to help you.

When I started teaching college pastoral classes, I developed the concept of a series of steps leading toward ministry. It began as a chart and grew into a booklet that my pastoral students read. That material has been adapted for this book because it can help young men who are curious about, interested in, or seriously considering pastoral ministry. Pastors, youth pastors, and parents can also use this material to help young men who are thinking about ministry.

What are the first steps from your initial thoughts about ministry to the day you are called to a church? Let's walk through them together.

PART ONE
Getting Started

CH. 1 ▶ My Path to Ministry

Do you remember your first thought about ministry? I remember mine. I was in high school, a sophomore I think. "I would never want to be a pastor," I thought. That's funny now, because I became one.

You might have thought positively about pastoral ministry, not negatively, like I did. Your thoughts might be described as mere curiosity. Or you may desire to be in vocational ministry. Possibly, you first thought about it when someone asked, "Have you thought about going into the ministry?"

Once you have those first thoughts about ministry, questions probably pop into your head. "What do pastors do?" "Would I even know how?" "How do I know if God wants me to be a pastor?" These are natural questions. Anyone would have them. I hope that what you are about to read will provide answers.

Let me share a little of how God directed me into ministry.

When I was eight years old, a friend witnessed to me about Jesus dying for my sins. Soon after, I believed on Jesus to save me. As a teenager I attended a Christian school and sang in the choir. Our choir traveled to churches in the area to present a program in which I narrated a part. I quoted a few verses of Scripture and repeated memorized lines that tied the verses to the song we were about to sing.

Several times people from the audience made comments like, "You sound great. You should be a preacher!" I seem to remember it was usually little old ladies saying such things. I didn't pay much attention, just thanked them and smiled.

My senior year in high school, when we were planning our senior trip, our class sponsor asked me to give a devotional message on the Sunday we were away. That was the first time I had ever studied a passage of Scripture and shared what I had learned with other people. I was extremely nervous but really enjoyed it.

When I finished high school, my family moved. After our U-Haul truck had been loaded, my parents had me drive ahead to the motel where we spent our first night while they cleaned and closed up the house. As I drove, all alone in the truck cab, I prayed. Words of surrender to God came from my heart. I told

God I wanted to do His will and asked Him to show me what it was.

From that time on, I experienced a steadily growing burden to be a pastor. I especially wanted to preach and teach the Bible. My pastor recommended a Christian college that trained men for ministry. I studied there as a Bible major with a minor in Greek (the original language of the New Testament).

After graduation, I attended seminary. During college and seminary, I was given opportunities to serve in churches, where I really enjoyed teaching and preaching. I discovered that the ministry of the Word was my passion and gift.

During my last year of seminary, a pastor contacted me about serving as a youth pastor. I had not known until then what I would do after graduation. God opened a door for me to be a pastor! I served there for four years, teaching and discipling teens.

My pastor generously gave me opportunities to preach to the whole church. These experiences cultivated in me a desire to preach to a broader audience. He encouraged me to be open to pastoring a church.

I was contacted by a church of about seventy-five people who were looking for a pastor. My wife and I visited there, I preached and answered their questions, and they voted to call me as their pastor. Again, God opened the door. At thirty-one, I became the pastor of a church!

I'm sharing my story with you to encourage you. If you're having thoughts about being a pastor, but you wonder if you'll be able to do it, I can reassure you that with God's help you can. If you are meant to be a pastor — as in, God wants you to be one — you will learn what you need to know, and God will give you the ability you need. He doesn't leave you on your own to figure it out for yourself.

In fact, the Bible gives many instructions for pastors. They are especially contained in the section of the Bible called the Pastoral Epistles. These are letters written to men in ministry, Timothy and Titus. The Pastoral Epistles are 1 and 2 Timothy and Titus. You can read these and learn some of what a pastor does. Additional specific instructions are given in 1 Peter 5:1–4. We'll talk more about these later.

What should you do if you are curious about the ministry or if someone suggests that you think about it?

You should take those thoughts and suggestions seriously. God uses our hearts' desires to guide us when we are yielded to Him.

He also uses other people who recognize in us gifts we don't realize we have. These people who know us can also help us discern whether we are motivated by selfish ambition or if we truly want to please God.

Pray and make yourself available to God. Tell Him you want to do whatever pleases Him and fulfills His will. If you are struggling with being willing to serve Him, be honest with your Heavenly Father. Tell Him about your struggle and ask Him to help you with it.

Another step you can take is to talk with your parents. Share with them the thoughts you're having. Parents provide wise input and can help you know how to process what you're experiencing.

A conversation with your pastor would also be worthwhile. He will be glad to know you're thinking about ministry and will give you helpful advice as well.

Take these initial steps as you consider the pathway to pastoral ministry. Be assured God will not leave you wondering what to do. If He wants you on this path, you will know. He will make the steps plain before you. Just follow Him.

Think and discuss.

Have you trusted Jesus Christ as your Savior? When and how did this happen?

What thoughts are you having about ministry?

What questions are you having about ministry?

CH. 2 ▶ Taking Your First Steps

Since you're still reading, I'm guessing you want to know more steps you can take on the pathway to pastoral ministry. Let's talk about three basic steps.

Read relevant Scripture.

An important and helpful basic step is to read sections of the Bible that are relevant to becoming a pastor. Here are a few suggestions. The first two relate to seeking God's direction. The rest are about the ministry.

Romans 12:1–2

Psalm 25:1–10

Acts 20:28

Ephesians 4:1–16

1 Timothy 1:12–14

1 Timothy 3:1–7

1 Peter 5:1–4

You might want to read a different passage each day for a week. Think about each one and how it impacts you. Journal your observations and thoughts. Pray for God to use His Word to guide you. You may encounter parts you don't understand or that you want to learn more about. You can explore them using a commentary or study Bible or ask your pastor to explain them to you.

If God is directing you toward ministry, these passages will probably intrigue you. You will want to understand more of what pastoral ministry involves. You might even feel excited about the possibility.

Pray for God to direct you.

Prayer is another basic step as you think about pastoral ministry. If you haven't prayed much before or you aren't sure what to pray about, now is a good time to learn. The Bible provides examples of how to pray. Let's look at two examples that will help you pray about God's direction for you.

The first is Psalm 25:4–5, one of the passages for reading suggested above. It contains several requests about knowing what to do when there is no specific biblical command that can guide the reader. You can adopt these words or rephrase them in your own way. Express them to God in prayer.

> Make me to know your ways, O LORD; teach me your paths.
> Lead me in your truth and teach me, for you are the God of
> my salvation; for you I wait all the day long.

The second passage is Colossians 1:9–10. This was Paul's prayer for others. You can pray it for yourself.

> And so, from the day we heard, we have not ceased to pray
> for you, asking that you may be filled with the knowledge
> of his will in all spiritual wisdom and understanding, so as
> to walk in a manner worthy of the Lord, fully pleasing to
> him: bearing fruit in every good work and increasing in the
> knowledge of God.

God doesn't hide His will from you! If He wants you to be a pastor or in a similar ministry vocation, He will make it clear to you. These prayers communicate to Him that you are open to His direction and are eager for Him to show you. As David said in Psalm 25:9, "He leads the humble in what is right, and teaches the humble his way."

Connect with your pastor.

You may have noticed I repeatedly encourage you to spend time with your pastor. Communicating with him is an important step on the pathway to pastoral ministry. Scripture shows us that God uses men already in ministry to identify qualities in those who will become pastors and to enlist them in ministry.

Paul did this for Timothy. He speaks of it in 1 Timothy 4:14, saying to Timothy, "Do not neglect the gift you have, which was given you by prophecy when the council of elders laid their hands on you." In 2 Timothy 1:6 he says something similar: "For this reason I remind you to fan into flame the gift of God, which is in you through the laying on of my hands."

The laying on of hands indicated recognition of God's call of Timothy. Paul and other leaders in the church formally affirmed that call. They observed Timothy's life, knew his character, and recognized qualities that enabled him to serve in ministry.

In the same way, church leaders today recognize and affirm God's call on a man's life and his readiness to serve in ministry. This is why it's important for your pastor to know you and to take part in preparing you for ministry.

You might think your pastor is too busy with important work to take time with you. Most pastors, however, are thrilled when a young man wants to talk about going into ministry. Sure, your pastor has a lot to do, but if you initiate getting together, he will likely be glad to do it. Some churches have multiple pastors. If this is the case in your church, you might feel comfortable connecting with a youth pastor or other assistant pastor.

A good place to start is just a conversation. Invite him to have coffee with you, your treat. Share with him your thoughts and questions about ministry. Ask him to pray for you and advise you. Let him know that you are available to help in the church and would like to learn about ministry.

As you get more involved in the church, stay in touch with him. Update him periodically on how you are thinking about future ministry. Ask him questions about various situations you face. Invite him to point out areas in your character where you need to grow.

If God directs you further along the pathway to pastoral ministry, this relationship will encourage you and assist you along the way. You may develop relationships with other pastors or ministry leaders as well. Cultivate and maintain these connections. Continue to ask for prayer, seek input, and update them on your progress.

Think and discuss.

What stands out to you from the Bible passages in this section?

How has praying about ministry helped you?

Have you discussed your interest in ministry with your pastor?
What does he think about it?

CH. 3 ▶ Getting Involved

One of the simplest steps you can take as you consider becoming a pastor is to get involved in ministry. "Ministry" is not just the name of a profession. It is serving. To minister is to serve. Some ministry activities may seem insignificant or mundane. However, even the small things are ways to serve God, help the church, and bless others. God gives more responsibility to those who are faithful in small tasks.

There are ways you can serve in your church right now. Getting involved in ministry will help you know whether it is your life's calling or not.

Talk with your pastor or other church leaders and offer to help in any way. You may be asked to serve in practical ways, such as greeting, ushering, or setting up for events. You might even be asked to share a testimony, give a short message, or visit someone with your pastor.

If your church conducts Vacation Bible School or something similar, that is a great time to experience ministry. Likewise, some Christian camps have teens and young adults serve as counselors. Volunteer for a week or more.

If your church has small group settings, such as life groups or community groups, get involved in one. Even if not many guys your age attend, give it a try. The church body connects in these settings, and you will discover opportunities to serve other believers. If you're unsure how to get involved, ask the group leader.

These are all good ways to taste ministry. They also enable people around you to observe you. These people may encourage you to pursue further opportunities to serve, which can indicate that you are meant for a life of ministry.

Think and discuss.

How are you serving in your church?

Are there other ways you would like to get involved in your church?

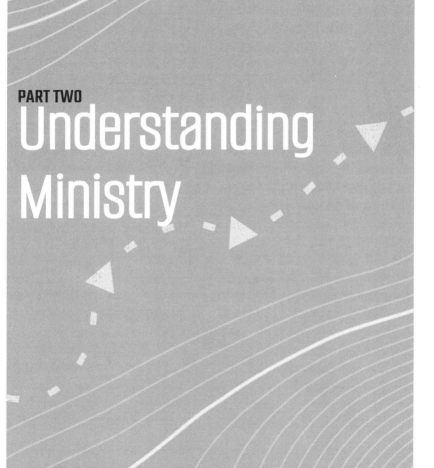

PART TWO
Understanding Ministry

CH. 4 ▶ A Pastor's Ministry of the Word

If you're thinking about being a pastor, you should learn what a pastor does. How does a pastor spend his time? What are his primary responsibilities? The work of a pastor can be divided into three categories. Pastors minister the Word, care spiritually for people, and lead and oversee the church.

The first area of a pastor's responsibility is the ministry of the Word. You might immediately think of preaching. This area definitely includes preaching, but there's more. The pastor's ministry of the Word is both public and personal.

A pastor's ministry of the Word is public.

Ephesians 4:11 links the word "pastors" (or "shepherds") with "teachers." The work of a pastor includes explaining and applying the Bible. Paul told Timothy to "preach the word" and to "reprove, rebuke, and exhort, with complete patience and teaching" (2 Timothy 4:2). Elders (another term for pastors) "labor in preaching and teaching" (1 Timothy 5:17).

A pastor may spend ten to twenty hours a week preparing to preach. Studying the Bible occupies a lot of time in his schedule. Pastors work hard to understand the meaning of Bible passages and to communicate the meaning and application in a way that is clear, interesting, and helpful to people.

A pastor may also teach a class or lead a Bible study. Some pastors preach or teach three to four times in a week. That requires a lot of studying! A faithful pastor will pray for guidance and enabling power as he prepares to deliver his message.

A pastor's ministry of the Word is also personal.

Paul described his ministry of the Word with the people in Ephesus as "teaching you in public and from house to house" (Acts 20:20). His approach to ministry included "admonishing every man and teaching every man with all wisdom, so that we may present every man complete in Christ" (Colossians 1:28). Pastors follow this pattern, explaining the Bible in person to families and individuals, encouraging them to trust and live by its truths.

A pastor's personal ministry of the Word includes sharing the gospel with unbelievers and discipling and counseling believers. He will explain sections of the Bible and help people understand difficult spiritual concepts. He uses the Bible to help those who are struggling with conflicts, temptation, and sin, showing them how to apply the truths of God's Word to themselves.

You can learn about preaching.

Let's circle back to preaching, because it's a big part of what a pastor does. You can take steps to learn about preaching right now.

- Listen attentively to good preaching. Take notes on the content of each message. Also observe how the preacher structures his message. You can even pay attention to how he uses his voice, face, and body language to communicate effectively.

- Learn as much as you can about the Bible. Read through it. You might want to start with the New Testament; then read the Old Testament. I find *Nelson's Book of Bible Maps and Charts* very helpful in getting the big picture of what the Bible is about. This book includes background information and an outline for every book of the Bible. A good study Bible can be very helpful as well.

- Make yourself available to give challenges, devotionals, and short messages. Let your pastor or student ministries pastor know you'd like to have opportunities to share the Word. Go ahead and work on a message even before you're asked to give one.

- Ask your pastor to show you how to put together a simple Bible message. When you're given an opportunity to speak, prepare diligently and pray for God's help. Enjoy the opportunity and learn from it.

These steps will give you an opportunity to experience this important part of pastoral work. By learning and doing, you will find out if you like it and if you are gifted at it.

Think and discuss.

Have you read through the entire Bible? Would you like to set a goal of reading through it, either for the first time or again?

If you had an opportunity to give a Bible message, what passage would you choose? Start studying that passage and write out word meanings, key words, and the passage's impact on you.

CH. 5 ▶ A Pastor's Spiritual Care for People

Another of the pastor's primary responsibilities is spiritual care for people. The word "pastor" actually means "shepherd." A pastor cares for his people like a shepherd does his sheep. Peter instructed pastors to "shepherd the flock of God which is among you" (1 Peter 5:2).

What does a pastor's care for his people include? First, he cares for their spiritual growth. A man named Epaphras is a good example. Many think Epaphras was the pastor of the church in the city of Colossae.

He visited the Apostle Paul, and Paul wrote to Epaphras's church members back in Colossae. He included this statement: "Epaphras, who is one of you, a servant of Christ Jesus, greets you, always struggling on your behalf in his prayers, that you may stand mature and fully assured in all the will of God" (Colossians 4:12).

This verse tells us a few facts about Epaphras. He had the people on his mind. He prayed fervently for them. And he wanted them to grow spiritually. These same characteristics are true of a good pastor. He has his people on his mind and heart, so he brings them before the Lord in prayer. And his goal for them is that they would mature in Christ and do God's will.

Opportunities to provide care for God's people come through the normal life of the church. A pastor interacts with his people individually before and after services, learning how they are doing and encouraging them. He conveys his heart for their spiritual growth in the way he leads the gatherings of the church, in the way he prays publicly, and through the applications he includes in his preaching.

A pastor will want to get to know his people. Paul, for example, described Epaphras, mentioned above, as "one of you." And Peter addressed his instructions to "the elders [pastors] among you" (1 Peter 5:1). These descriptions imply that these men spent time with their people and were not isolated from them. Part of being a pastor is getting to know people through visits and conversations, over meals in his home or theirs, and even by having fun together.

A caring pastor will use the circumstances of people's individual lives to encourage them and help them grow spiritually. The birth of a new baby, special family occasions such as birthdays and anniversaries he's invited to attend, graduations, and other significant milestones are opportunities to show interest and "rejoice with those who rejoice" (Romans 12:15).

A pastor also enters people's lives when they are hurting. He practices the "ministry of presence" when his church members are sick, having surgery, lose a loved one, or go through other difficult trials.

A pastor often visits people going through hard times, expressing comfort and praying with them. He encourages them to trust God for strength and to realize how God is working in them through these difficulties.

Have you or your family been helped by a pastor's personal ministry to you during a difficult time? If you have, you know how helpful it is to have a shepherd providing comfort, prayer, guidance, and assistance. It reminds you that God cares for you and has a purpose in the trial. Although it isn't always easy to walk with people through challenging times, a pastor is used of God in a great way.

If you're thinking about being a pastor, you might want to ask your pastor if you can go with him sometime when he visits people in the hospital or in their homes. You can observe how he shows care, brings comfort, and points them to God's purpose in trials. You might find you have a desire in your own heart to help people in the same way.

Think and discuss.

Do you remember a time when a pastor showed personal care for someone in your family or people you know who were going through a hard time? What did he do? How did he help or encourage them?

CH. 6 ▶ A Pastor's Leadership and Oversight of the Church

What does a pastor do? He ministers the Word both publicly and personally. He gives spiritual care to people. And he leads and oversees the church.

One of the terms used in the New Testament to refer to the pastor is "overseer." Or you might see the older word "bishop" in some Bible translations. "Overseer" is a good literal translation of the original New Testament word. The word in Greek is *episkopos*.

If you separate it into two parts, you get *epi* and *skopos*. *Epi* means "over." *Skopos* means "to see," like with a scope. The whole word means "to oversee." Part of a pastor's job is to oversee the church.

First Timothy 3:1 says, "If anyone aspires to the office of overseer, he desires a noble task."

First Timothy 5:17 says, "Let the elders who rule well be considered worthy of double honor, especially those who labor in preaching and teaching." The word "elders" is another term for the office of pastor. To "rule well" is to oversee.

Peter instructs pastors to "shepherd the flock of God that is among you, exercising oversight" (1 Peter 5:2).

As an overseer, a pastor provides leadership to the church. Pastors give direction to the ministry and guide it as an organization. They make plans that reflect the church's mission and lead the church in pursuing those plans. They equip and enlist people in various positions of responsibility.

A pastor is often the person up front, leading the service when the church gathers for worship and instruction. He also oversees by protecting the church from false teaching, corrupting influences, and division.

Some people are natural leaders. Not all pastors, however, feel comfortable and confident in a leadership role. Many of the qualities and practices of a leader can be learned. And, of course, God enables us to do what we could not otherwise do.

Seeing all these responsibilities may be overwhelming. But you may also have a growing interest and want to learn more.

Remember, if God wants you to be a pastor, He will enable you to do it. Yes, it's a lot of responsibility and hard work, but you will learn, and God will give you wisdom and strength to do it.

Think and discuss.

What do you think about being a leader? What are some ways you can grow in your leadership ability?

CH. 7 ▶ The Call to Ministry

You might have heard someone talk about the "call to ministry." If so, you naturally wonder what it is and how you know if you're called. The best way you can know is to understand what it isn't as well as what it is.

You don't hear a voice. You won't see a vision. Likewise, a sense of obligation because of the need for pastors isn't a call. Neither is a high-pressure call to action from a well-meaning preacher. Just because your dad and his dad were pastors doesn't mean you should be one.

The call to ministry is a realization that God is directing you into vocational ministry. This realization is accompanied by your own desire. And it is confirmed by church leaders who observe your character and gifts for ministry. To say it another way, if you think God is directing you toward ministry, you have a strong desire to be in ministry, and leaders in your church confirm you have the character and gifts for ministry, then most likely God is calling you into ministry.

Do you want to know something surprising? The Bible doesn't actually use the term "call" regarding pastoral ministry. But we see four elements in Scripture of God leading a man into pastoral ministry. These elements are realization, desire, qualification, and confirmation.

How do you know if you are being called?

You will have a growing realization that God is directing you into ministry.

In Acts 20:28, Paul instructed the pastors of the Ephesian church, "Pay careful attention to yourselves and to all the flock, in which the Holy Spirit has made you overseers, to care for the church of God, which he obtained with his own blood."

Do you see the word "overseers"? It's the word we talked about earlier that refers to pastors. The term "to care for" in this verse is a translation of the word meaning "to shepherd," which means "to pastor." So this verse is talking to pastors.

Notice Paul said, "the Holy Spirit has made you overseers." God actively worked in these men's lives directing them into pastoral ministry! They knew the Holy Spirit had led them into the ministry.

Earlier we talked about praying for God to lead you and being yielded to His will. If you submissively pray for God's direction, He will show you what to do regarding ministry.

Paul wrote, "For all who are led by the Spirit of God are sons of God" (Romans 8:14). This means anyone who is God's child will be led by the Holy Spirit to do His will. If God wants you to be a pastor, He will lead you to do it. You will realize God wants you in ministry.

You will probably ask, "How will He lead me?" Keep reading!

You will develop a strong desire to serve in ministry.

In 1 Timothy 3, Paul explained to Timothy how to identify men who should serve as pastors. Verse 1 says, "The saying is trustworthy: If anyone aspires to the office of overseer, he desires a noble task." There's that word "overseer" again, which refers to a pastor's leadership role.

See the word "aspires"? Some guys aspire to be professional athletes. Others aspire to go into the military or to construct buildings or to run a business or to teach. If you aspire to do something, you have a strong interest in it. When you think about your future, you envision yourself in that role.

Do you have a growing interest in being a pastor? Do you find yourself thinking about it when you consider your future?

A man who is called to ministry will aspire to it, but he will experience an even more compelling internal force. Paul's language goes to another degree of intensity in 1 Timothy 3:1: "he desires a noble task."

To "desire" means "to have a strong passion for it." If you are called to ministry, your initial interest will grow into a compelling passion. Being a pastor will not just be one option of several. You will not be able to see yourself doing anything else.

This desire may come on you suddenly, or it may grow progressively. But eventually you will find yourself saying, "I want to be a pastor." You will feel compelled.

Desire by itself, however, is not the call to ministry. There is another essential element.

Your life will evidence character that qualifies you for leadership.

Let's stay in 1 Timothy 3. Read over what Paul said in verses 2–7:

Therefore an overseer must be above reproach, the husband of one wife, sober-minded, self-controlled, respectable, hospitable, able to teach, not a drunkard, not violent but gentle, not quarrelsome, not a lover of money.

He must manage his own household well, with all dignity keeping his children submissive, for if someone does not know how to manage his own household, how will he care for God's church?

He must not be a recent convert, or he may become puffed up with conceit and fall into the condemnation of the devil. Moreover, he must be well thought of by outsiders, so that he may not fall into disgrace, into a snare of the devil.

These characteristics are often referred to as "qualifications for ministry." A man who desires to be a pastor must have these qualities. He will not exhibit them perfectly, but a person looking at his life would say he definitely fits this description.

This description might intimidate you or seem overwhelming. Yes, the standards for a pastor's personal life and character are high. But these are traits any young man should cultivate. If your heart is open to God's work in you, He will enable you to grow in these qualities.

Read over these qualities repeatedly. Look up each word in a dictionary, or ask a parent or your pastor to help you study them. Journal your thoughts about each one. Pray for God to help you become this kind of man.

With God's help, resist temptations that take you away from these qualities. Choose friends who encourage you to live in these ways.

Whether you go into pastoral ministry or not, you will mature over time into a godly man. Your life will glorify God, and you will influence others for Him.

How do you know if you are being called to ministry? You will realize God is directing you toward ministry. You will have a strong desire for ministry. You will develop character essential for spiritual leadership. Here's one more essential element.

Leaders in your church will confirm it.

We're still in 1 Timothy 3, where Paul told Timothy how to evaluate men who were interested in ministry. If interested men were qualified, Timothy would confirm their qualification. Today God still uses leaders in the church to observe men's lives and confirm their readiness for pastoral ministry.

Timothy's call to ministry, for example, was publicly confirmed by a group of pastors. Paul later encouraged Timothy, "Do not neglect the gift you have, which was given you by prophecy when the council of elders laid their hands on you" (1 Timothy 4:14).

In 2 Timothy 1:6 Paul spoke of his own personal involvement in confirming Timothy's call: "For this reason I remind you to fan into flame the gift of God, which is in you through the laying on of my hands."

In both letters Paul said that he and others laid hands on Timothy. The laying on of hands showed formal recognition that Timothy was qualified for ministry. Paul, along with other church leaders ("the council of elders," 1 Timothy 4:14), confirmed that Timothy was ready to engage in pastoral work.

Just as church leaders confirmed a man's readiness for ministry in the first-century church, pastors in your life will do that for you. If you are supposed to be a pastor, leaders in the church will recognize character and gifts in you that qualify you.

Stay in close touch with the pastors around you. These men will observe your life and help prepare you. When the time is right, they will formally confirm that you are qualified, gifted, and ready for pastoral work.

These four elements of a call to ministry will not all happen at once. They will unfold in your life over time. If you have an interest in being a pastor, it will grow into a strong desire. As you open your heart to God's leading, you will sense He is directing you toward ministry. You will mature as a Christian man, and the qualities in 1 Timothy 3 will develop in your life.

Your pastor and other leaders in the church will encourage you toward ministry. You will be given opportunities to preach and teach. People will be impacted by your care for their souls. You, your spiritual leaders, and the people of God will know that you are called to ministry.

Think and discuss.

Which of these best describes you?

- I don't know if I am supposed to be a pastor, but I'm open to it.

- I think God may want me to be a pastor, and I want to learn more.

- I have a strong desire to be a pastor.

How can you develop the qualities listed in 1 Timothy 3:2–7?

What does your pastor think about your interest in ministry?

CH. 8 ▶ Feelings of Inadequacy

You might hesitate to pursue being a pastor because you feel inadequate. The role and responsibilities of a pastor seem too great for you. You're not sure you should be explaining the Bible to people. You are just starting to understand it yourself! You are reluctant to try to help other people overcome sin. You have your own sin struggles! You hear a pastor preach, and you can't imagine yourself ever being able to preach like that.

Feelings of inadequacy are normal. In fact, if you think you can do ministry with your own natural ability, you are probably not viewing it correctly. Ministry is human activity, but it is also a result of the supernatural work of God. **He enables you to do what He calls you to do**.

The Apostle Paul wrestled with his own inadequacy to minister the gospel. He said, "Who is sufficient for these things?" (2 Corinthians 2:16).

God makes you sufficient.

We can be thankful Paul didn't stop there. A few sentences later, he answered himself, saying, "Not that we are sufficient in ourselves to claim anything as coming from us, but our sufficiency is from God, who has made us sufficient to be ministers of a new covenant" (2 Corinthians 3:5).

It's true—you *are* inadequate, but God makes up the difference. He enables you to do what you can't naturally do. If God wants you on the pathway to pastoral ministry, He will help you each step of the way.

One of my favorite prayers in the Bible was prayed by King Jehoshaphat when he was about to be attacked by a million-man army of enemy nations. In desperation and dependence, he said, "We do not know what to do, but our eyes are on you" (2 Chronicles 20:12).

I've often prayed in a similar way as a pastor. The responsibilities are greater than I am, and I face many issues where I don't know what to say or do. I just pray, "God, this is way beyond me. But I'm trusting You to help me." He always does. He will do the same for you.

Think and discuss.

How does the truth that God will make you sufficient help you with feeling inadequate for ministry?

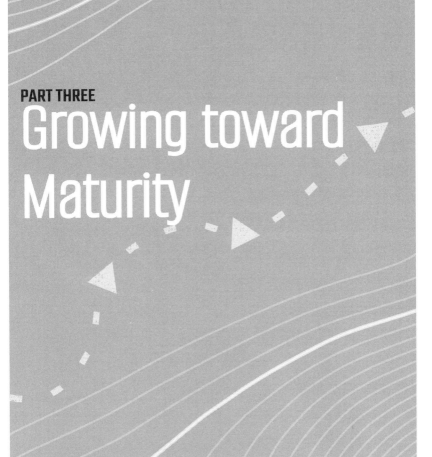

PART THREE

Growing toward Maturity

CH. 9 ▶ Growing in Character

Pastors are men of character. Some jobs don't require a man to be honest, morally pure, and humble. Most professions have no expectation for a person's marriage or family life. In contrast the instructions in Scripture hold pastors to a high standard.

Don't, however, let the character requirement scare you off. If you are a Christian growing in the Lord, you are able to meet these qualifications with God's help. But you must be serious about it.

You have to recognize and admit your weaknesses. You must be willing to develop new thought patterns, attitudes, and habits that reflect godly character. And you must protect yourself in areas where you are vulnerable to temptation and a lack of self-control.

You are establishing patterns right now that will stay with you for life. You are becoming who you will be in ten years. What kind of person are you?

Are you lazy or diligent? Proud or humble? Greedy or generous? Self-centered or considerate of others? Do you indulge in impure imaginations, or do you fight to keep your thoughts pure? Do you follow others into foolishness and sin, or do you stand firm on doing what is right? Do you love yourself, or do you love God? Do you serve your own interests, or do you serve God and others?

If you're a Christian, God is already at work in you, showing you that you need to grow. Remember, developing godly character is not just for pastors. Every Christian is growing. Whether you're going to be a pastor or not, you will glorify God by growing in your character.

What is character? It's who you are as a person. It isn't about your outward appearance, though your character will affect how you look. Character is the real you. It's what you are inside. Character makes you do what you do when no one is telling you what to do.

The Bible provides examples.

The Bible is full of examples of character, good and bad. Often you'll see a person in Scripture who has both good qualities and weaknesses. That's human nature!

One example is David. As a young man he was a shepherd. His job included guarding the sheep from hungry predators. First Samuel 17:34–35 says he fought a lion and a bear who wanted to have lamb for dinner. David's character included dependability and courage.

Then David's courage went to another level as he faced Goliath with a handful of rocks and a leather sling, but the source of his courage was a deeper motivation. Goliath had "defied the armies of the living God" (1 Samuel 17:36). David cared more about God's glory than his own life. With God's help, he defeated the giant. Read the whole story in 1 Samuel 17.

David became king. He fought and won many wars, all for the cause of God. However, as with every man alive, including you and me, he had a weakness. Being a man of character includes knowing your weaknesses and protecting yourself from falling. David had a weakness for a beautiful woman.

Although he was a married man, he looked, lusted, and indulged his desire for a woman who was not his wife. Second Samuel 11 and 12 tell this sad tale. Thankfully, David recognized his sin and received God's forgiveness, but much damage had been done: many people were affected by his actions, and David's leadership was never the same.

We can learn powerful lessons from both the good and the not-so-good elements of David's character. He was known as a man after God's own heart (1 Samuel 13:14). David displayed devotion to God and bravery against enemies, and he was motivated by a great cause.

But he also failed to protect himself where he was vulnerable. He gave in to temptation. He committed a great sin. David's life shows us not only good character but also the importance of guarding our character.

As you read through the Bible, look for examples of others like David. Notice how the heroes of the faith related to God, how they showed faithfulness to Him, and how they failed. Learn from them the kind of man to be and the kind of man not to be.

A pastor's character matters.

By now you've looked at the list of qualities in 1 Timothy 3:1–7. Did you look up definitions? Discuss them with your pastor? If not, take some time to do that. Remember, even if you don't know you'll be a pastor, these are qualities any young man should develop.

Do any of the characteristics in 1 Timothy 3:1–7 stand out as areas where you need to grow? Be honest. Are you weak or vulnerable in any areas? Where are you likely to be tempted? Do you have an area of your life that Satan could use to hinder you from being a young man with godly character?

Where you've failed, ask and receive God's forgiveness. His grace is greater than your sin: "Where sin abounds, grace abounds much more" (Romans 5:20).

This is a good time for a conversation with your parents, a good friend, and your pastor. Ask these people to point out areas of character where you need to grow. Be honest about areas of vulnerability, and ask people to pray for you. See if they can recommend any helpful resources for overcoming sin struggles.

God is at work in you.

Ultimately, godly character is produced by the Holy Spirit in you. Another place in the Bible that instructs us about godly character is Galatians 5:16–24.

Verses 19–21 list character traits produced by our sinful nature.

- The first three have to do with sexual thoughts and acts outside of God's plan for marriage: immorality, impurity, and sensuality. (A few versions list these as four.)

- The next two involve worshiping and seeking power from gods other than the one true God: idolatry and sorcery.

- Several of these traits involve conflict and animosity with others: enmities, strife, jealousy, anger, disputes, dissensions, factions, envying.

- The last two involve alcohol and partying: drunkenness and carousing.

Let's move now to the list of godly character traits, those produced in you by the work of the Holy Spirit: love, joy, peace, patience, kindness, goodness, faithfulness, gentleness, self-control.

The Holy Spirit produces these traits of godly character in you. This happens when you yield to Him and expose your mind and heart to the truth of His Word. So it's important to read the Bible regularly (ideally every day!) and choose to submit yourself to be the kind of person God wants you to be.

You don't have to manufacture godly character. God is at work inside of you, cultivating character traits that will show up in your life. You're not on your own! He will enable you to be the kind of man who can serve in pastoral ministry.

Character determines influence.

Godly character is essential to spiritual leadership. Paul told Timothy, "Let no one despise you for your youth, but set the believers an example in speech, in conduct, in love, in faith, in purity" (1 Timothy 4:12). That instruction is for you too! Develop character so people will take you seriously.

Paul also urged Timothy, "Keep a close watch on yourself and on the teaching" (4:16). Pay attention to your own life first: your walk with God and your character. Then you can teach others.

A pastor is not a super saint, but he is serious about developing and protecting his own character so he can influence others. Ultimately, godly character is Christlikeness. Every Christian should develop attitudes and actions that resemble Jesus. Growing in character is not just one step; it happens all along the pathway to pastoral ministry.

Think and discuss.

Ask someone close to you these questions: What are my character strengths? What areas do I need to work on?

Who stands out to you as an example of good character in the Bible? Why?

How is God at work in your life, developing godly character in you?

CH. 10 ▶ Growing in Knowledge

A major step on the pathway to pastoral ministry is expanding your knowledge. You might be overwhelmed thinking about more learning after you graduate from high school.

Think about it this way. Any meaningful career requires training. If you're going to be an electrician, you spend years learning the trade. To become an engineer you have to go to four years of college. Becoming a doctor requires college, medical school, and residency. This takes ten years or more!

Pastors are in a sense doctors of souls. If years of education are necessary for a secular profession, how much more should you be willing to invest time, effort, and even finances to gain the knowledge and skills necessary to be a pastor?

Your church is the first place to learn God's Word. Some churches even provide formal teaching that prepares men for ministry. Bible colleges and seminaries are designed to provide in-depth instruction by professors who have dedicated their lives to their fields of study so they can equip men for ministry.

A good Bible education develops biblical understanding.

If you attend Bible college, you will take some classes that survey the entire Old Testament or New Testament in one semester. Others dig deeply into single books of the Bible, such as Genesis, the Psalms, Matthew, Acts, Romans, Ephesians, and Revelation. Each book has a specific message and contains key truths. As you grow in your understanding, you will be able to help others learn and live by the Bible too.

Learning the original languages of the Bible will help you understand it so you can explain it to others. Pastors should at least have a working knowledge of Greek so they can translate from the New Testament. Hebrew, the language of the Old Testament, is more challenging, but it helps to have even a basic understanding of how it works.

Classes that focus on pastoral skills will help you learn to preach, to disciple and counsel, and to lead the church effectively. Even general classes such as English, science, math, and history equip you to relate to others and to communicate clearly and accurately.

Consider these three biblically-based reasons.

Why should you further your education after high school if you're going into ministry? The Bible doesn't specifically say you have to go to college and seminary, but here are some points to consider.

First, you mature a lot between ages 18 and 25. Your character, understanding of life, and ability to influence people develop during these years. The qualities we looked at earlier listed in 1 Timothy 3:1–7 require time to mature. Challenges and temptations that come with a few years of adult life prove a young man's character. The time you spend in school learning the Bible and growing in pastoral skills also allows you to mature into a godly man ready to minister to others.

Second, one of the required qualities of a pastor is "able to teach" (1 Timothy 3:2). When you graduate from high school, are you ready to explain to all the members of a church the various truths of the Bible and how they apply to life? Does your depth of Bible knowledge enable you to deliver sermons every week to a congregation made up of children, teens, young adults, and men and women older than you? The years you invest in a

Bible-focused education will equip you to preach and teach the Word to the broad spectrum of people in a congregation.

Third, your motivation should be to please God, not yourself. If you're going into ministry, you can't shirk hard work because you don't feel like doing it. Paul instructed Timothy, "Do your best to present yourself to God as one approved, a worker who has no need to be ashamed, rightly handling the word of truth" (2 Timothy 2:15).

The term "do your best" can also be translated, "Be diligent." In other words, work hard! Why? "To present yourself to God as one approved"; that is, to honor God. This is the ultimate goal of every Christian, and it is the number one reason to go into ministry. We don't earn God's favor. He accepts us because we are in Christ, but we do please or displease Him with how we live. According to this verse, we can please Him by being diligent in our work.

Second Timothy 2:15 goes on to say what kind of work Paul was talking about: "rightly dividing the word of truth." He challenged Timothy to put in the hard work necessary to handle the Word of God correctly. God's Word is worthy of all the labor we invest in understanding it. We honor God by our accurate presentation of its truths to others.

This would be a good time to have another conversation with your pastor. Treat him to a cup of coffee. Ask him what he thinks about the best way to pursue education that will prepare you for pastoral ministry. Likely, he will have a few suggestions for you.

Education is hard work! But the people you will one day minister to will thank you. And your Lord Jesus Christ is worthy of your best efforts.

Think and discuss.

What educational options are your parents and pastor recommending to you for ministry preparation?

Have you considered any colleges? If so, what do you think about them? If not, should you plan a college tour?

PART FOUR

Developing Skills

CH. 11 ▶ Speaking Skills

With any vocation, a set of skills is necessary to do your work. Is this true for pastors too? Doesn't God enable a pastor to do his work? Yes, He does. He makes you able to do what you could not do in your own knowledge and strength. But there is a human side to pastoral work as well. Preparing for ministry includes growing in your understanding of how to do pastoral work and in your skill at performing it.

When Paul instructed Timothy about the qualifications of a pastor in 1 Timothy 3, he said, "These things I write to you, though I hope to come to you shortly; but if I am delayed, I write **so that you may know how you ought to conduct yourself in the house of God**, which is the church of the living God, the pillar and ground of the truth" (1 Timothy 3:14–15, NKJV, emphasis added). Paul encouraged Timothy to learn how to function in church life. This instruction applies to you as well.

What I mean by "pastoral skills" is not so much things like how to preach, how to share the gospel, and how to perform a wedding. Of course you need to learn these too. What I'm talking about here are finer points of conducting yourself in your pastoral responsibilities. Let me explain.

We've already discussed three primary areas of a pastor's responsibility: the ministry of the Word (public and personal), spiritual care for the people, and leadership and oversight of the church.

Pastoral skills are connected to those areas of responsibility. The three kinds of pastoral skills I will focus on are speaking skills, people skills, and leadership skills. You can begin developing these skills now. You will grow in them as you continue on the path to pastoral ministry. In fact, you will mature in these your whole life.

Let's start with speaking skills. We'll address the other two in chapters 12 and 13.

We've already talked about taking steps to learn to develop and deliver sermons. You can do this with your pastor before you start formal training, and you will have classes on preaching in college or seminary. But let's think more broadly than just preaching.

Pastors are, by nature of their work, communicators. As a pastor you will do a lot of speaking in front of a group of people.

That might scare you. It does most people. Public speaking ranks high on the list of people's greatest fears. But you can grow in your confidence and in your ability to speak to groups. When you have something important to say, you can overcome your fear and nervousness.

My purpose here is not to give speech lessons. I'm going to highlight areas to focus on and give a few words of advice as you learn to communicate effectively with a group of people.

Learn to prepare thoroughly so you know what you're going to say.

This applies to everything from announcements to sermons. If you have something to say, you'll be able to get it out when you're in front of a group of people. Think through the details you need to communicate. Select the best wording. Jot notes down so you will remember. Use these as a cue sheet when you speak.

Learn to format your content for effective communication.

When you're speaking to a group of people, you want to connect with them personally. You're not an audio book reader or a scientist sharing research data. You're speaking from your mind and heart to theirs.

Whether you're preaching a sermon, welcoming attendees to a service, or introducing a speaker, be warm and personal. Think about the people you're going to be speaking to as you prepare to speak. Your notes may look good on paper, but how will the words and ideas sound as you verbalize them out loud to real live people? Don't just offload information. Communicate.

Learn poise.

This third area might strike you as a little weird. That's okay. Just think about it and let it grow on you. I'm not talking about walking with books on your head. Poise is an appropriate confidence in stressful situations. I would describe it as **overcoming your discomfort to put others at ease**.

You might feel awkward standing in front of people. It's okay for people to know that, especially when you're starting out. But you need to quickly get over your discomfort because it distracts your listeners. If you are comfortable being up front, your listeners will be comfortable with it too.

Also, distractions and disruptions go with public speaking. Anything can happen. Cell phones ring. Babies cry. People walk out. (They're probably not mad at you, just going to the bathroom!)

The sound system squeals. If you let these rattle you, everyone gets uncomfortable and distracted. If you respond with patience and grace, and if you recover quickly from the disruption, everyone else will too.

Being comfortable in front of people doesn't mean you're overly casual. Plant your feet, stand up straight, and lift your voice. Your delivery conveys the significance of your message. If you're slouching all over the podium, mumbling, and fiddling with your phone, people won't take you seriously.

Poise also includes handling difficult matters with tact. As a pastor, you will speak to your flock about sensitive issues. At times the church will engage in a process of church discipline, and you will need to communicate with the congregation about it. There may be division in the church that you must address firmly but with grace. You'll need to develop wording for these occasions that deals with the problem as directly as needed but without causing people unnecessary embarrassment. The spirit you convey should reflect the seriousness of the situation but not be unduly harsh.

One more area of speaking skills to develop is creativity.

Here's the reality: pastors say the same things to the same group of people week after week after week. Sure, you preach a different sermon every week. But think about what else a pastor says during a 60–90 minute worship service.

> "Good morning everyone. It's a beautiful/cold/rainy day out there. Welcome to our church."

> "Here are a few announcements . . ."

> "Would the ushers please come forward to receive our offerings."

> "Turn in your Bibles to . . ."

> "You're dismissed."

People naturally lose interest when the same things are repeated using the same words. Using your imagination a little when planning what you're going to say will help them pay attention.

Even with your preaching, remember you're not just repeating information you found in a bunch of commentaries. You're communicating truth to transform people's hearts, minds, and lives. Take time to think about the best way to help them process that truth. Think of how Jesus used examples from nature, culture, and life to illustrate truth. Don't just say the first thing that comes to your head. Develop fresh wording for familiar ideas.

Don't, on the other hand, go overboard with creativity. Too much can distract people from the information you're announcing or the truth you're preaching. Just be interesting enough to get and keep their attention.

There's a lot more you will learn about speaking effectively in front of people. Pastors talk a lot! That's what shepherds do. Jesus said of shepherds, "The sheep hear his voice, and he calls his own sheep by name and leads them out" (John 10:3). He was illustrating His relationship with His people. He said, "My sheep hear my voice, and I know them, and they follow me" (John 10:27).

In a similar way, your people will get to know your voice. You will lead them by what you say. It's essential that you speak accurately and clearly so they will understand you. It helps to speak a little creatively so they'll continue to listen to you. Keep developing your speaking ability as you follow the pathway to pastoral ministry.

Think and discuss.

Do you have opportunities to speak in front of people? How can you develop as a speaker?

ᴄʜ. **12** ▶ People Skills

Another area of pastoral skills you will need to develop is people skills. Here are seven areas to grow in and work on.

A genuine love for people comes first.

Some people skills can be learned, but there must first be a genuine love for people in your heart. I was talking with a neighbor couple recently about my work. I explained to them that I am equipping a new generation of pastors. The sweet, elderly lady said, "Oh, they need to love people!" She's right.

Love for others starts with yielding to the Holy Spirit and allowing Him to produce this fruit in you. "The fruit of the Spirit is love" (Galatians 5:22). You can also learn to love people by following Jesus's example. We are to "walk in love, as Christ loved us and gave himself up for us" (Ephesians 5:2). Paul gave us an idea of what love looks like in ministry: "And I will very gladly spend and be spent for your souls; though the more abundantly I love you, the less I am loved" (2 Corinthians 12:15, NKJV).

Loving people means you don't minister to them for what they do for you. Rather, you give yourself to and for them because you want their highest good. This doesn't mean you're going to be close friends with everyone in your church. But you will care for each one. And you will serve and even sacrifice for them, just as Jesus did.

Develop your love for people by asking God to produce the fruit of love in your life. Read the Gospels (Matthew, Mark, Luke, and John) and observe how Jesus demonstrated love. Study the description of love in 1 Corinthians 13. Be alert to your own self-centeredness, and with God's help, intentionally replace it with love.

Be interested in others.

Loving others leads to a second people skill, developing genuine interest in people. We naturally think a lot about our own lives: what we're doing today, how we're feeling, what's going on in our family, our problems. Learn to look beyond yourself and be interested in others.

Pastors usually minister to a pretty large group of people. It takes intentional effort to learn about their families, their work, their activities, and their burdens. These life circumstances are the setting for spiritual growth. If you as a pastor wish to help your people grow spiritually, knowing about their lives is vital.

Here's a good daily reminder from Paul: "Do nothing from selfish ambition or conceit, but in humility count others more significant than yourselves. Let each of you look not only to his own interests, but also to the interests of others" (Philippians 2:3–4).

Become a conversationalist.

How do you show interest in other people? How do you get to know them? Through conversation. So the third people skill to learn is how to converse with people.

You may do this naturally, or you may need to develop conversation skills. Start by asking questions. "Tell me about your family." "What kind of work do you do?" "Where all have you lived?" "What do you do to relax or have fun?"

But don't make it seem like an interrogation. Hopefully, the other person will ask you questions too! If not, you can tell a little about yourself, or comment on what the person said, then ask another question. Ideally a conversation should be like tennis. You hit the topic "ball" back and forth to each other. If the other person asks you a question, answer it, then ask him or her a similar one. "I have three siblings—two brothers and a sister. How about you?"

Once you get to know people, you can move from small talk to more meaningful topics: "How did you become a Christian?" "What are some of the big lessons God has taught you?" "How can I pray for you?"

An essential step in getting to know people is doing things together.

This fourth skill is something you may not do naturally. You might need to make an effort and grow in your desire for it.

Some pastors hole up in their offices and escape to their own homes and never do anything with people in their church. Some even have the idea that they shouldn't develop friend-ships with their people. My answer to that is, look at Jesus. Of all the people He ministered to, He spent quality time with twelve. They hiked, ate, and had many conversations together. Just as Jesus spent time with His disciples, pastors can and should do the same with their church members.

The most basic thing you can do is visit them in their homes. But go beyond that. Invite some to your home for pizza and games. Include couples, singles, older people, and kids. Organize a bowling night or go to a ball game. Post on social media you're going for a hike and anyone is welcome. Have a dads and kids day at the park and invite some men to come along (the moms will love this).

These times can be planned or spontaneous. Doing things together lets people know you care about them as individuals. They also have an opportunity to see you're real and you like to have fun. You will find that investing this kind of casual time with people will develop relationships that give you opportunities for meaningful ministry to them.

Learn how to act in a considerate way toward others.

The fifth people skill is to have good manners!

Remember that stuff your mother taught you? It's important. If no one taught you manners, well, you can read up on them. Manners are just a way of being considerate of others. You're not putting on a show. You're putting others before yourself and showing that you care for the people around you.

Eat what you're served. Chew with your mouth closed. Use eating utensils properly. Cover your cough. Dress appropriately for the occasion. Don't be crude. Don't be on your phone unless everyone is doing phones. Express gratitude (say "thank you," and send a thank you note if someone has you for a meal or gives you a gift). Give a firm handshake (but not a bone-cruncher!). Stand up to talk to another person who is standing up. Ladies first. Hold the door. Practice proper netiquette. (Pastors can really hurt their ministry by being rude on social media.)

Society is becoming careless and crude, but etiquette shows that you care for others. You don't have to be stiff and formal. Just be warmly and thoughtfully polite. You will reflect Christ well and enhance your relationships with others.

Learn how to relate to people who are in difficult circumstances.

We naturally feel inadequate when we talk with someone experiencing the death of a loved one, loss of a job, or other hardship. If you haven't experienced it, you hardly know what to say. This is especially true when you are young.

You can always say, "I don't fully understand what you're going through, but I just want you to know I care for you, and I'm praying for you." Beyond that, you can learn by spending time with an experienced pastor. Observe how he interacts with people during a time of serious illness, accident, job loss, major surgery, family crisis, or death.

As you go through trials of your own, you will become more sympathetic with others who suffer. You will learn helpful things to say and do. You'll experience God's grace in your life and will be able to encourage others to trust Him for the measure of grace they need.

Experience helps, but most of all, pray for wisdom. Pastors are there for people during the most difficult of times. God will enable you to minister to others, even when you aren't sure what to say or do. Trust Him, show love, and provide support.

Learn how to relate to people who are different from you.

You're young, they're old. Or you're an adult, they're kids. You're one ethnicity, they're another. You're country, they're city. You've got degrees hanging on your wall, they don't. You grew up learning verses, they barely know how to find Matthew in the Bible.

You will need to learn to bridge many gaps between yourself and others. Here are a few quick ideas on how to learn to relate to different kinds of people.

One is to look for people you don't naturally gravitate to and initiate conversation with them. Just walk up and start talking (see above on being interested and having conversations).

Another is to expose yourself to various types of people through reading, listening to, and watching news and other sources of information. Look for programs, podcasts, and even read historical fiction that will give you a new perspective on how different kinds of people live.

One more. Travel. As much as you can, get out of your own geographical area and visit places where people different from you live. See the sights, eat the food, go to the shops. Sure, attend their churches too. As much as possible, expose yourself to different cultures, both within your home country and outside it. Interact with people with a vastly different culture from yours. You will grow to understand and appreciate the differences in background, perspective, and life experiences. This will help you relate in a new way to the amazing diversity of people on God's earth.

Here's a quick review of people skills to develop.

- Love people.
- Be genuinely interested in people.

- Converse with people.
- Do things together.
- Act in a considerate way (manners!).
- Relate to people in difficult circumstances.
- Relate to people different from you.

Guess what: there's no pastoring without people. You may love to study, have a passion to preach, and you can't wait to lead, but churches are people. Jesus died and rose again to save, set apart for Himself, and spend eternity with people!

Your ministry is to people. Developing people skills will enable you to fulfill your ministry, follow God's purpose, and build up the church of Jesus Christ.

Think and discuss.

What are two or three ways you would like to grow in your people skills?

CH. 13 ▶ Leadership Skills

In addition to speaking skills and people skills, pastors need leadership skills. If you're thinking about going into ministry, now is a good time to begin growing as a leader.

Leadership is the ability to influence people in a direction they need to go. Being a leader doesn't mean you are an aggressive personality, taking charge of everything and ordering people around. Leaders see the direction a group of people needs to go. In the church setting, the direction includes spiritual growth on an individual level and making disciples as a church. A leader communicates those ultimate goals to the people. He also encourages and equips them to pursue those goals.

A pastor, as a leader in the church, will often see steps a church can take or strategic efforts it can implement to pursue the goal of reaching its community with the gospel and making disciples. A pastor will intentionally provide teaching and urge the people to do their part. Or he may see ways in which the church needs to mature as a body, so he preaches from passages of Scripture related to those areas and plans ways the church can apply these truths together.

How can you develop now as a leader?

Pray for God to develop your leadership.

Jesus developed the disciples. They were normal men who became influencers. He taught them, gave them opportunities to serve, corrected them when needed, and eventually entrusted them with starting the first churches after He ascended back to heaven.

In a similar way, God will enable and develop you into the leader you need to be to fulfill His purpose for you. Express your dependence on Him through prayer. Ask Him to give you wisdom, help you learn from experience, and mature you into a man who can influence others.

Learn from others who lead.

You can do this by reading good resources on leadership. A great book to start with is *Spiritual Leadership* by J. Oswald Sanders. I recommend it very highly. Sanders tells you what it means to be a spiritual leader, gives many helpful principles, and includes a lot of examples. It truly is a life-changing book.

You might want to read and discuss it along with someone else—your dad, your pastor or youth pastor, or a friend.

Also, observe how your pastor and others in positions of influence exercise leadership. Watch how they lead a group of people to pursue goals. Observe how they communicate. Notice how they plan, then enlist and equip others to pursue the plan. Pay attention to how their example affects others.

You can even learn from leaders' weaknesses and mistakes. I don't mean to encourage you to have a critical spirit, but sometimes leaders handle things in a way that isn't the best. Quietly make a mental note of what they did and the impact it had, and think of how you might handle it differently if you were in their place.

Learn from Jesus.

Jesus is the greatest leader of all. Read through the Gospels (Matthew, Mark, Luke, and John), paying special attention to how Jesus influenced others and what He taught His disciples about leadership.

Carefully read Mark 10:35–45. Jesus's disciples asked Him for prominent positions in His kingdom. He responded by telling them that God views greatness very differently from how the world views it. His words have become the gold standard for leadership in Christian ministry:

> You know that those who are considered rulers of the Gentiles lord it over them, and their great ones exercise authority over them. But it shall not be so among you. But whoever would be great among you must be your servant, and whoever would be first among you must be slave of all. For even the Son of Man came not to be served but to serve, and to give his life as a ransom for many. (Mark 10:42–45)

You can learn Christlike leadership by letting these words shape your life. Pray that the quality of selfless service will be formed in your heart and will determine how you relate to others.

Seek opportunities to get experience.

In your church setting, gaining experience may include helping plan and execute events, assisting with Vacation Bible School, or being on a youth council. You may also have opportunities at your school with class offices, special events, athletics, or clubs. If you have a part-time or summer job, look for ways to go beyond just putting in your time. Take extra responsibilities, help with planning, or develop a new idea to improve the business.

Leadership can be learned.

Some people's natural personalities or abilities make them leaders. You may not feel that's you, but anyone can acquire knowledge, gain experience, and develop leadership skills. And when God wants you to influence others, He is at work from within, growing you so He can use you in Christ's church-building work.

If you are supposed to be a pastor, God will enable you, and you will learn to lead. Think of it like a shepherd with his sheep. He knows they need food, water, and protection. The shepherd thinks ahead, knows where to take the sheep for nourishment and safety, gets out in front, and starts going in that direction. His sheep follow him.

As a pastor, you will need to get out front. You don't have to act like a military commander or a corporate CEO. Just start pursuing spiritual growth and bring others with you.

I love this passage from *Spiritual Leadership*, the book I mentioned earlier:

> Leadership is often viewed as the product of natural endowments and traits of personality – intellectual capacity, force of will, enthusiasm. That such talents and scholastic attain-

ments do greatly enhance leadership is beyond question, but those are not the factors of paramount importance in the spiritual leader. **The real qualities of leadership are to be found in those who are willing to suffer for the sake of objectives great enough to demand their wholehearted obedience**. (emphasis added)[1]

If you obey God's call on your life and His commission to make disciples, and if you are willing to spend your life serving Him, you will influence others in the same direction. You will become the leader you need to be.

---

1   J. Oswald Sanders, *Spiritual Leadership: Principles of Excellence for Every Believer* (Chicago: Moody Publishers, 2007), 25.

Think and discuss.

What are some ways you would like to grow in leadership?

PART FIVE

Looking Ahead

CH.
14 ▶ What Is Ordination?

What does the word *ordination* make you think of? Maybe you imagine a solemn ceremony where men wearing black robes touch you on the head with a scepter and pronounce you "Reverend." Or you see yourself seated alone at a massive table while scholars of divinity gleefully examine you with tricky theological questions. Possibly you have no idea what ordination is as it relates to pastoral ministry.

Ordination is a significant milestone on the pathway to pastoral ministry.

I want to help you understand ordination so you can anticipate and prepare for it. You won't find in the Bible the word *ordination* in relation to men becoming pastors, but a biblical practice is the basis for ordination. Bible-based churches today practice ordination in a way that follows this pattern.

When a man is ordained for ministry, pastors who know him affirm that he is qualified, gifted, and ready to serve as a pastor.

The ordination event usually includes a formal examination by an ordination council. This council consists of pastors and other ministry leaders who are themselves ordained.

These men hear the candidate's testimony of being saved and called to ministry. The candidate presents a written statement of biblical doctrines, and council members ask him questions about it. They may also question him regarding his views on current issues.

If the council determines that the man is ready to begin serving as a pastor, they will make this recommendation to his church. The church then makes it official in a special ordination service. This usually involves a "laying on of hands" ceremony by church leaders.

First Timothy and Titus contain the examples we follow in our practice of ordination.

First Timothy 3:1–7 describes the kind of man who is qualified for pastoral ministry. Paul's instructions to Timothy imply that Timothy was supposed to decide whether other men were qualified for ministry. Similarly, the process of ordination is intended to determine and confirm that a man is qualified for ministry based on his character, understanding of the Bible, and gifts.

In Titus 1:5 Paul instructed Titus "to appoint elders in every town as I directed you." Then he gave Titus a list of qualifications (1:6–9) mirroring those in 1 Timothy 3. So again we see that spiritual leaders in the church are to evaluate and confirm that a man is ready for ministry.

First Timothy 4:14 speaks of an event in Timothy's life. Paul encouraged Timothy, "Do not neglect the gift you have, which was given you by prophecy when the council of elders laid their hands on you." The "council of elders" was a group of pastors who formally affirmed Timothy's giftedness and readiness for ministry. They signified this affirmation by the act of laying their hands on Timothy.

Pastors who know you will be the natural ones to ordain you.

Ideally pastors will be involved in your life during the years leading up to your ordination. They may help you by pointing out areas where you can grow and by giving you opportunities to learn ministry so you will be ready for ordination. Stay in close touch with the pastors you know.

Anticipate ordination like a graduation.

If you are considering ministry, you shouldn't worry about ordination, but you can anticipate it. A healthy respect for the significance of this event is appropriate. When the time comes, you will be ready. Ordination will be an occasion for you and those who have invested in you to recognize and celebrate God's faithfulness and grace in calling you to ministry.

Think and discuss.

Have you ever attended an ordination?

If so, what do you remember about it? If not, talk with your pastor about attending one when there is an opportunity.

CH. 15 ▶ Called to a Church!

One day you may receive a message that looks something like this:

> Your pastor gave me your name as a possible candidate for a pastoral position in our church. If you are interested, please send your résumé, doctrinal statement, and testimony of your salvation and call to ministry. We look forward to hearing from you.

Nothing could be more exciting if you've been on the pathway to pastoral ministry!

The experience of being called to a church may vary for different individuals. But here are a few common practices that will help you know what to expect.

Someone will express interest in you as a possible candidate for a pastoral position.

He will likely be the pastor of a church who needs help with shepherding responsibilities. It may be your home church's pastor, or the pastor of a church you serve in while in college or seminary. It might be a pastor you don't know who was given your name.

You may even be contacted by a deacon or pulpit committee member of a church who needs a lead pastor. Smaller churches especially will sometimes call new seminary graduates as their pastor, so don't be surprised by this contact if you've been serving faithfully and have exhibited growth in pastoral skills while in school.

Some schools have a ministry placement service. When you're about to graduate, you can upload your name and profile information so churches looking for potential candidates can find you. This can be a good way to connect with a church. In my experience, however, your contact with churches is more likely to happen through the network of people who know you.

Pastors you know will play a very important role in your being called to a church.

You may be asked by one of your mentors to serve as a pastor with him. Or a pastor friend may give your name to a church looking for a pastor. The pastors who know you best will provide a reference for you. They will testify to your character and faithfulness to a church that is considering you. They will pray for God to lead you and open doors of opportunity for you. And they will be a source of counsel as you consider opportunities.

Your first position as a pastor will probably be in an assisting role.

An assistant's role may involve general responsibilities of helping the lead pastor oversee and care for the church. Or it may be a specialized area of responsibility, such as students or discipleship, or a combination of several areas of ministry.

If both you and the church are interested, you'll start sharing information with each other.

They'll want to see your résumé, a statement of your doctrinal beliefs, and your testimony of being saved and how God led you into ministry. You should ask for the church's doctrinal statement, bylaws, and a written description of the role you are being considered for.

The next step is an interview.

An interview may take place by phone or video call or in person. There will be lots of questions! The church leadership will want to get to know you. Be ready with some questions of your own too.

If all is positive, the church will invite you for a visit.

This visit may be a get-acquainted time, or it may be an official event for you to candidate. You'll meet with church leaders and key people in the ministry area that you would be serving in. You'll most likely preach or teach. And you'll answer more questions.

By this time both you and the church will have a pretty good idea of how you want to proceed. One of the leaders (the pastor, pulpit committee chairman, or deacon) may say, "We would like to have you come be our assistant pastor. If our church votes to call you, would you come?" You may know, or you might need to think and pray about it to make a final decision. If your answer is yes, the church will schedule a business meeting and the members will vote.

Your phone is buzzing. "We just finished our business meeting. Our church members voted to call you! Will you come?"

Congratulations. You've just been called to a church. You're a pastor!

Think and discuss.

Take a few minutes to pray for God to lead you in His will regarding ministry and to help you prepare for His calling on your life, whatever it may be.

Ask your parent(s), your pastor, or a friend to pray for God to direct you as you seek His direction about ministry.

Equipping pastors to be confident and skilled in specialized areas of ministry

Don't go through 4 years of college for a generic pastoral degree. At Faith, you choose a targeted and focused area of study that fully prepares you to minister confidently in areas based on your interests!

With Faith's Pastoral Studies Program, you can get your pastoral degree with an emphasis of study in the following areas:

Biblical Counseling | Expository Preaching
Greek | Music and Worship
Organizational Leadership | Youth Ministries

LEARN MORE AT
faith.edu/academics/pastoral-studies

 faith baptist bible college and theological seminary